Recommended

The Bible says without fa[...] please God. This means in order to live a Godly life, we must trust God to be who He has promised us He is, and then walk in that knowledge. In Pastor Frank Thompson's book, 50 Days of Faith, we learn that fear is the enemy of faith. To live the life God promised, we must trust God to walk us from fear to faith; to be the believers He has called and equipped us to be. This book is a must read for every child of God who desires results in their Christian walk. Read it, meditate, and watch your faith come alive and your life transform.

Pastor Michael C. Bradford
Changing Lives Ministries

50 Days of Faith

Refusing To Doubt, Overcoming Fear & Celebrating Breakthrough

Frank L. Thompson

All Scripture quotations and paraphrases are taken from the King James, NASB and Living versions of the Holy Bible; and are intended to help guide you to pray prayers that are taken from God's Holy Word.

Faith Days of Faith – Refusing to Doubt, Overcoming Fear and Celebrating Breakthrough

ISBN: 978-1-312-93529-7

Request for information should be addressed to:

Frank Thompson Ministries
Harvest Church – St. Louis
6301 Garfield
Berkeley, MO 63134

Contents

Introduction
Refusing to Doubt

If your faith is being tried, just know that this season is designed to produce a greater understanding of God's love, so why doubt God now? God wants to make sure that your level of faith exceeds the intensity of your trial, so he allows that measure to be tried so you may see what level of faith that it is. With this in mind we must remember that we are here in this trial, going through this test at this very moment to discover his unfailing love, experience his wonderworking power, and overcome another level of fear. God loves us enough to leave us where we are until we are equipped for the next victory, so never give up on victory. Remember that the boldness and confidence that you need tomorrow, is hidden in the trials that you are facing today; so why doubt God now?

Overcoming Fear

What are you secretly afraid of? In these troubled times are you secretly afraid of losing your job, home or car? Are you afraid of losing your credit rating, afraid of late charges, or is Satan oppressing you with the fear of debt, sickness, death, and divorce or losing your family? If so,

I have good news, for God has delivered all of us who through fear have been subject to bondage. He has delivered us from the power of darkness and has translated us into the kingdom of his dear Son. The power of darkness is simply the spirit of fear. This weapon of choice for Satan has been responsible for the captivity of God's people who do not walk in this truth. The spirit of fear is an ungodly spirit seeking worship and is a snare and stumbling block to our faith and total victory. Today the spirit of fear has masqueraded itself as the fear of man or man made things such as the fear of not enough, and it has disguised itself so that it can blend in to our everyday life. However, God has not given us the spirit of fear to associate with, but power, love and a sound mind. It is the mind of Christ which always speaks wholesome, healthy words of faith. The Bible clearly says that the fear of man brings a snare, but whoever puts his trust in the Lord shall be safe. Overcoming fear in your life is a skill that David the shepherd boy had to gain before making it to the palace. Even though the palace was his place of destiny, he had to first kill the lion, the bear, and the Goliath in his life. The same goes for you, you will first have to kill the lion in your life if you are going to make it to the palace. The lion in most of our lives is none other than the spirit of fear. It is Satan who goes about as a roaring lion, seeking who he may devour. We live our lives in our thinking, so in order to overcome fear we must think faith. When you believe God with the absence of doubt, unbelief, and fear, it will always bring you total victory and total power. Total faith will lead you to the place that God designed for you to live and glorify him in this present world. Perhaps you are saying I know that I am saved, but still I find myself fearful and struggling to believe almost every day. How do I get to the place where I have total faith, total power, and total victory over the spirit of fear? How do I finally rid myself of the fear in my life? Well, one of the most profound things that you can ever learn is that fear only works on those who are trying to save their lives! That's why Jesus said "whoever will come looking for me let him deny himself, take up his cross and follow me. For whoever will save his life will lose it; but whoever will lose his life for my sake and the gospel's the same shall save it."

Have you ever noticed that young people don't seem to be afraid of the police? Aren't you bewildered and wonder why radical extremists and suicide bombasts are not afraid of dying? The answer is this, **YOU CAN'T INTIMIDATE DEAD PEOPLE!** We live our lives in our thinking and if you are already dead, then fear has no power over you. You see, there is a point in our trials that the power of God is activated in our mortal bodies, a point in which fear has no hold. A point where we realize that the snare of fear is broken and we have escaped. We must remember that we died with Christ on Calvary and that our funeral took place at baptism. The Apostle Paul said it this way, I am crucified with Christ, nevertheless I live, and yet not I, but Christ lives in me; and the life that I now live in the flesh I live by the faith of the son of God, who loved me and gave himself for me.

Celebrating Breakthrough

One of the most profound revelations that can ever be discovered is the fact that **your breakthrough is not the issue**. The conflict is over worship because this is what causes us to rejoice in tribulation, and take pleasure in our infirmities. God has designed his people to go to a place of victory and triumph through worship. For if God can ever get his people to worship him he can release the promises. The conflict that you are in is over the celebration of truth and the voice of triumph. All of God's people need to be broken again in order to worship in spirit and in truth. When God's own people won't worship him it is the face of rebellion. The fact is that all of God's people who don't worship have been taken captive and live in bondage. So in order for breakthroughs to start manifesting, judgment must start at the house of God so that we can get a head start on brokenness. The church today really doesn't know what real brokenness is until they worship. For true brokenness releases the power of God in your home, finances, and your church. **God wants us to push up not give up.** He wants us to push the weight of our trials up and become exercised thereby. Don't worry about being weak, because God wants your strength to run out and allow his strength to run in. The place that God is taking us to will not work with your religious mind, nor will it work if we are walking by sight. In other words, God wants to get the world out of our eyes. Sometimes God says things that do not excite you but you still need to worship. The natural mind cannot understand what God is saying in the natural, but worship instantly gives us understanding through the spirit. Now the things that are impossible with men is possible with God, as a matter of fact all things are possible with God. He wants us to believe that our breakthrough is not just possible but available. His divine power has made all things available to you that pertain to life and Godliness. The time to celebrate your breakthrough is now, because that which is to be hath already been! At one time the Lord was not your God and you had no hope, no covenant, and no promise. However, God has deposited into your account everything that pertains to your breakthrough, and the only thing missing is the celebration.

Faith Is

1.   Faith is the evidence itself of what is being hoped for and needs no further proof in order to begin worship.

2.   Faith is the life and promises of the spirit being experienced now and walked out in the natural.

3.   Faith is the life of the new creature flowing into our thoughts.

4.   Faith is a request by the King of Kings and the Lord of Lords to come into his presence.

5.   It is the gift of God and the invitation by which we are allowed to come boldly to the throne of grace.

6.   Faith is the foundation of everything that God has to offer, and is the means by which he dwells in our hearts.

7.   Faith gives us access to the promises of God and this is the victory by which we overcome the challenges and tests of this world.

8.   Faith comes by hearing and this ability to hear comes by hearing God speak through his word.

9.   Faith occurs while we are responding with praise and obedience to what we have heard.

10.   It is the substance of everything that we hope for and the proof that we have what we heard him say.

11.   Faith is the shield by which we quench all of the fiery darts of the wicked and works by understanding His love.

12. Faith means that you are not focusing on the things that are seen, but on the unseen things that he has said.

13. Faith is an act of obedience putting us on a mission from God and that mission is to obey him.

14. Faith is the power of obedience in operation proving that you believe what he said.

15. Faith is God's way of thinking or his way of achieving success.

16. Faith is now, faith has already experienced victory, and faith never struggles.

17. Faith is actually God talk or talking on the God level, for without it you cannot communicate with him.

18. Faith is operated by the knowledge of God's love.

19. Faith is the outspoken expression of love in your heart toward God.

20. Faith is your response to his love and sacrifice.

21. When you cash your check they give you the exact amount for which it is written, even so faith is the exact match for your need.

22. Faith is not a function of the human spirit, but an anointing to ask and believe.

23. Faith is simply taking advantage of every opportunity to speak God's word into the atmosphere against the challenges of your life.

24. Faith is in the unseen power of God, and victory in advance before the battle is even fought.

25. Faith is the victory that overcomes the world because faith is victory.

26. Faith is unique in that it has nothing to do with the natural.

27. Faith is made up of supernatural words that we use to describe what we see in the spirit.

28. It is the building material of those who believe for the supernatural.

29. Faith is the kingdom conversation of believers or a kingdom conversation with the king.

30. Faith is our way of asking God for the things that he bled and died to give us.

31. It is the way of access given by God to ask him for the things that are freely ours.

32. It is the language of the Holy Spirit or the language of the kingdom.

33. Faith is the evidence that believers look for who are speaking his language and acting on God's word.

34. Faith is a demonstration of God's attributes.

35. Faith activates the power of God and gives him permission to act on your behalf.

36. Faith is the realm that celebrates what God has done today.

37. Faith is having a kingdom mentality and providing a godly response to your problems and tests.

38. Faith is the realm of the now, and the switch that turns God's power on.

39. Faith is based on what we know about the love of God.

40. Faith is spiritual genius because it calls things which be not as though they were, then adds corresponding actions that cause manifestations to take place.

41. Faith is a vision from God of you accomplishing your goal.

42. When you have faith you are simply laying claim to something that God has already provided which means that something that you were hoping for has now become yours.

43. Faith is the voice of his word.

44. Faith is having an unquestioning belief that needs no further proof or evidence.

45. Faith says about itself what it discovers about God, for as He is so are we.

46. Faith can never be anything other than victory.

47. Faith works by love and love is always a process.

48. When God's promise introduces his plan, it stirs up faith's potential.

49. Whenever the victory of faith is declared, defeat is not an option.

50.   Faith comes because you recognize that it is God talking.

Day 1

A Time to Worship

But the hour cometh, and now is, when the true worshippers shall worship the Father in spirit and in truth: for the Father seeketh such to worship him. (John 4:23)

One of the first rules of achieving success in life is to know what time it is. Not just what time it is in the natural, but it is even more important to know what time it is in the realm of the spirit. Time is the period between two events or during which something exists, happens, or acts. It is that measurable interval that is available for something to take place. Therefore it is vital that you know when it is time to worship. Whenever you find yourself in between what you desire and the manifestation of that thing, you know that it is time to worship. First of all worship is the first fruit, and the fulfillment of purpose. It means engaging in prayer, supplication, and thanksgiving in order to summon the presence of God. It is also the interruption of pain, heartache, or trouble to exalt God and give him the glory that is due his name. Worship is the relationship that you have been trusted with and also means to walk in submission to the purpose, will and plan of God. So if you are in between manifestations of victory and breakthrough, start speaking to yourself in psalms and singing spiritual songs. This is a perfect time to make melody in your heart to the Lord, until what you are longing for in the spirit shows up in the natural.

Faith is the evidence itself of what is being hoped for and needs no further proof in order to begin worship.

Day 2

A Time to Worship 2

If a man die, shall he live again? all the days of my appointed time will I wait, till my change come. (Job 14:14)

It is time to worship because things are about to change. So please know that whenever you worship things will change and wherever you worship God is where the change will take place. Please be advised that whatever trial and whatever test that worship occurs in is destined for a miracle. So don't be fooled just because things don't manifest immediately.

To everything there is a season, and a time for every matter or purpose under heaven. God has a purpose for what seems to be delay. Remember that delay is a mechanism of time and time always has a purpose. Delay is a mechanism of time used to fulfill the plan and purpose of God. We must learn how to wait upon the Lord and look for him. He will soon reveal the deep and secret things as to what, when, why and why not. You are soon to find out that he knows exactly what is in the darkness, and the light dwells with him.

Faith is the life and promises of the spirit being experienced now and walked out in the natural.

Day 3

Absolute Faith

But let him ask in faith, nothing wavering. For he that wavereth is like a wave of the sea driven with the wind and tossed. For let not that man think that he shall receive any thing of the Lord. (James 1:6-7)

There is a kind of faith that causes you to receive whatever you ask God for that is called absolute faith. This faith is pure, undefiled, and never fades away. It contains absolutely no fear, unbelief, or doubt and is a very present help for us whenever we are in trouble. Its strength is unmatchable because it is stronger than sickness, or death, and even life itself. It is stronger than angels, principalities, powers, things present, things to come, and yes it is stronger than everything that is against you. Absolute faith boasts in righteousness because it brings healing, deliverance, liberty to the captives and will always set us free. This faith is the prize of both heaven and earth, for it makes us steadfast under pressure, unmovable in trials, and when we are knocked down, it causes us to get up and abound in Christ. It's like having hinds feet, or four feet causing us to walk in places of influence and high places of authority with seemingly no reason to be there. This kind of faith enables us to cast down evil imaginations and everything that exalts itself against the knowledge of God. Absolute faith is absolutely fearless. Fear has no power against it and is reduced to mere shadows in its light. Danger is no longer a threat and must find a place to retreat. This faith brings joy unspeakable, is indescribable and causes us to overcome things that are insurmountable. Now the best thing about absolute faith is that it is already in your heart.

Faith is the life of the new creature flowing into our thoughts.

Day 4

Absolute Faith 2

Now we have received, not the spirit of the world, but the spirit which is of God; that we might know the things that are freely given to us of God. (1 Corinthians 2:12)

Even though you are being tried you need to know what has been freely given to you. You may feel strengthless, without courage, and even feel fearful. However, you should also know that God has given you a measure of absolute faith for your particular trial. He will never allow you to suffer or go through more than you have faith for. This measure of faith that he has given you is more than enough for what you are facing, and is a down payment of absolute faith for the next trial. You see, we go from this level of faith which is born of God to more absolute faith. For whatsoever is born of God overcometh the world: and this is the victory that overcometh the world, even our absolute faith. Absolute faith is already victorious, and will completely overcome all of your trials, tribulation, and circumstances. There is no defense against this kind of faith, for it is greater than anything that will ever come against you. It can remove mountains, change situations, and call things into being as though they have always been. When we are sick, absolute faith produces healing, and in trouble it gives us deliverance and reveals our way out. Always keep in mind that if God spared not his own Son but delivered him up for us all, doesn't it make sense for him to freely give us all things?

Faith is a request by the King of Kings and the Lord of Lords to come into his presence.

Day 5

Absolute Faith 3

But what saith it? The word is nigh thee, even in thy mouth, and in thy heart: that is, the word of faith, which we preach (Romans 10:8)

Satan works overtime to keep you from discovering something that you already have called absolute faith. It is already in your heart and in your mouth. Absolute faith is the gift that comes from hearing God's word. This is why the enemy hopes that you never fall in love with the word, because this is exactly how all of your needs are met. They are met through this absolute faith of the kingdom which is hidden in you. Now if what you need cannot be found in the kingdom of God, it does not exist. God simply supplies all of our needs from the riches of the kingdom which can be seen through absolute faith. When we talk about absolute faith, we are talking about an unquestioning belief in God and his power that does not require further proof or evidence. This kind of faith is never far from you, and is always ready to go to work. So always remember that whatever is in your mouth and in your heart is in your hands. All you have to do is speak and it will go to work in you and for you. Now God knows exactly what you have, what you need, when you need it, and where it is going to come from! He knows that what you are looking for will only be found within! For God still delivers, sets free and makes ways to escape when there is no way. All you need is absolute faith! Now fear works by understanding the danger of this world because fear is a god of this world. However, the spirit of absolute faith in you is much greater than all of the fear that is in the world. Please keep in mind that when you have absolute faith, it works by understanding the love of God. Now when this knowledge of God becomes mature, it casts out all fear. Absolute faith also creates a peace that passes all understanding, because this kind of faith is the voice of God's word. This is the reason why anything that God says cannot come back void of fulfillment because his voice is in what he says. So if you are going to walk in complete victory over fear, all you have to do is worship Him in absolute faith.

It is the gift of God and the invitation by which we are allowed to come boldly to the throne of grace.

Day 6

Absolute Faith 4

Sometimes when we are going through intense trials and tests, we cannot seem to find that very thing that produces a vision of victory called absolute faith. Now it is important to realize that God hid what you are looking for in Christ so that Satan would not have access. Furthermore, we have this treasure inside of us; it just seems to be lost at the moment. However, I have some good news, for this is precisely why Jesus has come. The Son of Man has come to seek and to save that which seems to be lost. So please know that you can always find faith in your trial if you know where to look. His strength always makes its debut and comes to its total potential in our weaknesses. This is why you should count your trial as joy which is the strength of his people. The trying of your absolute faith develops confidence in God's timing and prepares you for greatness at the top! Remember that whatever you actually believe God for in absolute faith will not be overdue, not even one day. Now the just shall live by absolute faith which is exactly how you got saved. You were saved by grace through absolute faith. This faith that you got saved by has already taken up residence in your soul forever and is not going to leave. The Lord Jesus himself dwells in our hearts by faith and he said that he would never leave or forsake us. He has in fact declared that you belong to him, and not even Satan himself has enough power to claim what belongs to God.

Faith is the foundation of everything that God has to offer, and is the means by which he dwells in our hearts.

Day 7

Absolute Faith 5

And the devil, taking him up into an high mountain, shewed unto him all the kingdoms of the world in a moment of time. And the devil said unto him, All this power will I give thee, and the glory of them: for that is delivered unto me; and to whomsoever I will I give it. If thou therefore wilt worship me, all shall be thine. And Jesus answered and said unto him, Get thee behind me, Satan: for it is written, Thou shalt worship the Lord thy God, and him only shalt thou serve. (Luke 4:5-8)

God has given every man power to believe called absolute faith. However, when we hear God's word and don't believe, it becomes absolute doubt! Wherever your thoughts are engaged gives the power of that faith unto Satan or unto God. Furthermore, whoever you submit absolute faith to will be the object of your worship. Jesus is the best example that we can see of absolute faith in action. Satan will always present you with a set of circumstances to see what you will do with them. Every situation stands before you for only one reason and that is to determine to whom you will give power, glory and honor. Power is yours to give to whomever you want to give it, so take your faith out of Satan's power and give it back to God. When we talk about power, it is the multiplication of a quantity times itself producing the right to rule. Power does not belong to the situation that you are facing; it does not belong to the sickness, affliction or lack. Power does not belong to the fear, loneliness, or depression. Power belongs to God, yes it belongs to your deliverance. The greatness, the power, the glory, the victory and the majesty of the situation that you are facing belongs to God. He is the greater one and the head of all principalities and power. So our faith should not be in the enemy's threat, or in our limited capacities to fix things but in the power of God. The deliverance that you need will not be overdue one single day, hour, minute or second. He is faithful and will supply everything that you need on time. God has raised you up in this situation so that he can display in you his power. He has in fact dashed in pieces every situation that you are facing, and has brought you out by his mighty power.

Faith gives us access to the promises of God and this is the victory by which we overcome the challenges and tests of this world.

Day 8

Power Belongs to God

God hath spoken once; twice have I heard this; that power belongeth unto God. (Psalms 62:11)

When it comes to power, it is special authority assigned to or exercised by a person or group holding office specifically, the Godhead. It is the manifestation of that authority in operation which God has delegated to us. Power belongs to God absolutely, because there is no power but of God. So let every soul be subject to the highest power, which no doubt is not Satan, but God himself. Now when it comes to our thinking, every thought is full of power. This is why the word of God discerns the very thoughts and intents of our hearts. Your thoughts determine whether God's power is limited or becomes manifested in our situations. Wherever your thoughts are engaged gives the power of that faith unto Satan or unto God. Even the spirit of fear needs the power of our thoughts to be effective...otherwise it has nothing to work with. We need to make sure that our power is always in the right hands. Power does not belong to the weakness that you are facing because he gives power to the faint and to them that hath no might he increases strength. Power does not belong to the lack that you face because God has given us power to get wealth. The powers that be as the Bible calls it or the power of our thoughts are ordained of God. Now if you want to see God work in your situation, you must not deny his power in your thinking. You must not fall into the category of those who have a form of godliness but deny his power an opportunity to work.

Faith comes by hearing and this ability to hear comes by hearing God speak through his word.

Day 9

God's Power

And it came to pass on a certain day, as he was teaching, that there were Pharisees and doctors of the law sitting by, which were come out of every town of Galilee, and Judaea, and Jerusalem: and the power of the Lord was present to heal them. (Luke 5:17)

God's power is synonymous with his presence, for where his presence abides so does his power to heal and deliver. His power is present wherever there is a need. For Jesus said, "I am come that they might have life, and that more abundantly." Notice that Jesus says "I am come", this is an announcement of triumph and greatness for our success. When Jesus Christ comes into your life, he brings with him all the victory of the cross, and declares that we are complete in him. Therefore, we are not without wealth, healing, peace, and not without victory; we are complete in him. He has taken everything captive that can hold us captive and has given us it's defeat as a gift. When Jesus came into our lives he did not come empty handed. Jesus Christ could not come into our lives until he had first defeated everything that could stop us from having life or else his coming would have been in vain. That's why he went to the cross so he could suffer in our place and overcome everything that we would ever face; that way we would not have to. Please get this. He suffered, bled and died on the cross for your current trial. So whatever your complaint is or may be, please understand that just as he bore your sins, you should also know that he also bore your griefs and carried your sorrows so that you would not have to. This means that we have overcome every obstacle and circumstance because he overcame it for us. Therefore, without him we can do nothing of ourselves.

Faith occurs while we are responding with praise and obedience to what we have heard.

Day 10

Answer the Call

We having the same spirit of faith, according as it is written, I believed, and therefore have I spoken; we also believe, and therefore speak; *(2 Corinthians 4:13)*

Now there is a spiritual law that declares that out of the abundance of the heart the mouth speaks, so we must say what we believe. When the enemy challenges us with a trial and calls us out for a fight, we must answer the call with the word of God. Some of you are in the fight of your life; just answer the bell! How many of you would ever let your child pet a dog who you knew was going to bite them? Or how many of you would give your child a pet that you knew was going to injure them. Well if you, who are earthly, know how to give good gifts unto your children, how much more shall your Father which is in heaven give good things to them that ask him? Always be aware that God has a plan to manifest to the world that we are actually his sons and daughters by manifesting his power in us. His plan is first to convince us of what he has already done. He wants us to be assured that he has already defeated and taken every trial captive and handed it to us as a gift. His plan is to take every trial captive by both infusing and confusing it with the power of his word. Every trial is an invitation to show up with God's word...because you will have what you say. Every trial is simply a call for God's sons to manifest themselves. The trial going on in front of you is simply a call to manifest the power within you. So answer the call!

It is the substance of everything that we hope for and the proof that we have what we heard him say.

Day 11

Answer the Call 2

But as many as received him, to them gave he power to become the sons of God, even to them that believe on his name (John 1:12).

Many of God's children today are facing financial difficulties and challenges. This is a trial calling for a word of abundance. Some are facing disease, affliction, and sickness, requiring a word of healing from the Son. Even more are facing marital and family problems, calling for a word of peace. Still there are others who have been in their trial for quite some time. Their tribulation is calling for a word of strength. Now the Word of God tells us that we have what we say; so the question is, what shall we then say to these things? For starters you can begin by saying "God is for me and there is no defense against him, and every force that is against me is defeated." Remember that you will get the benefit out of every spirit upon you. That spirit will anoint you whether good or bad. Just make sure you keep in mind that where faith lives, change will occur. This happens because the kingdom of God is not just in word only, but in divine power.

Faith is the shield by which we quench all of the fiery darts of the wicked and works by understanding His love.

Day 12

Answer the Call 3

And when they were come to the multitude, there came to him a certain man, kneeling down to him, and saying, Lord, have mercy on my son: for he is lunatick, and sore vexed: for ofttimes he falleth into the fire, and oft into the water. And I brought him to thy disciples, and they could not cure him (Matthew 17:14-16)

In this lesson, the disciples find themselves faced with a dilemma; it is a call to demonstrate power; the power of God within them. The task at hand was to cast out a devil and make this young man whole again. Whatever formula the disciples were using was simply not working. We now know that we must still abide in God's plan for deliverance even if we are his people. The scriptures also tell us that it is the spirit that makes what we say come alive. The will of the flesh profiteth nothing. However, Jesus said "the words that I speak unto you, they are spirit, and they are life". Always keep in mind that your trial is requiring that you think like God, talk like God, and act like God. We know this because when Jesus commanded the evil spirit to leave the child, the young man was made whole. Darkness may be the dominant theme in your life, but just remember that darkness covers everything in its path except the light. Jesus told us that his words were life and light. This light shines in the darkness, and the darkness comprehendeth it not. Last, but not least, please remember that wherever you can find a word to describe your trouble, you can also find a word to believe.

Faith means that you are not focusing on the things that are seen, but on the unseen things that he has said.

Day 13

Look in Your Mouth

But what saith it? The word is nigh thee, even in thy mouth, and in thy heart: that is, the word of faith, which we preach (Romans 10:8-11)

Looking for the right thing to say in your trial? The word you are looking for is already in your mouth and in your heart. Your mouth and your heart will always release what your trial is calling for through faith. This would be a very good time to declare that the words that you are looking for have already been found, and produce both joy and rejoicing in your heart. Your confession should always declare that "I have what this trial is calling for; I have what it takes". Allow me to reiterate that where faith lives, change will occur. By your words you will be justified, and it is by your words that you attract condemnation. The entrance of God's word gives us light; it gives understanding even to the simple. God's word releases joy, peace, happiness, strength, direction, money and abundance through faith. When we find the word, it causes us to rejoice as one that has found great spoil, or in our times rejoicing, like someone who has found a lot of money. Remember that God's word is a lamp unto our feet, and a light unto our paths. So don't worry about what you should say in your trial. The word of God promises in Matthew 10:19-20, that when we are delivered over to circumstances and trials, that words shall be given for us to speak in the same hour. Remember it is ultimately not you that speak, but the Spirit of your Father which speaketh in you.

> *Faith is an act of obedience putting us on a mission from God and that mission is to obey him.*

Day 14

The Importance of Prayer

And all things, whatsoever ye shall ask in prayer,
believing, ye shall receive (Matthew 21:22)

So why is prayer important and how do we know that it works? Prayer is simply asking, believing, and receiving what you need for our greatest educator, the School of Life. Prayer is in its simplest form, the privilege of asking in the will of God. Please keep in mind that Jesus said, "if you ask anything in my will, I will do it". Furthermore, the word declares that our confidence comes from knowing that we are asking in his will because he is listening to us. Now if we know that he is listening intently, we also know that we have whatever petition we have desired of him. So prayer is God's way of giving us the desires of our hearts. Therefore, we should keep in mind that prayer is also one of the greatest forms of worship. A man that does not worship, is a man that does not believe what the word says about the Father who is looking for true worshippers. Now prayer becomes effective when love is involved because it is simply the language of two parties in love. One party is so in love that he even sacrifices his own Son just to adopt us into his family. However, the second party is still learning how to love. We constantly ask ourselves what manner of love is this that God has bestowed upon us, that would make Jesus lay down his life for his friends. The answer is that this love of God is so vast and intense that it surpasses knowledge. So when God allows us to simply ask for whatever it is that we need, this becomes the proof of the importance of prayer in the kingdom and why faith really works by love.

Faith is the power of obedience in operation proving that you believe what he said.

Day 15

The Blessings of Obedience

But they that wait upon the LORD shall renew their strength; they shall mount up with wings as eagles; they shall run, and not be weary; and they shall walk, and not faint (Isaiah 40:31)

What is obedience? Our quest for obedience may be obtained quicker if we know what obedience is. Obedience is the single most important thing in your life, because it is something that you must hear in order to comply with what is being said. In summary obedience is simply a word, but what kind of word is it? Obedience is a word of faith that allows you to put your trust in God's discretion. Obedience is also a sacrifice, the putting aside of something valued for the sake of something else having a more pressing claim. To obey means that you value God's opinion, his instruction and his discretion over your own. Though it seems to elude you, please know that obedience is always in your mouth and in your heart because it is simply the word of faith. Now without faith it is impossible to please him: for he that cometh to God must believe that he is, and that he is a rewarder of them that diligently seek him. Therefore, obedience is something heard in the spirit that causes us to move! By faith Abraham, when he was called to go out into a place which he should after receive for an inheritance, obeyed; and he went out, not knowing whither he went. By faith Noah, being warned of God of things not seen as yet, moved with fear, prepared an ark to the saving of his house; by the which he condemned the world, and became heir of the righteousness which is by faith. What is God requiring for you to do, and where is he leading you?

Faith is God's way of thinking or his way of achieving success.

Day 16

Achieving Obedience

Though he were a Son, yet learned he obedience by the things which he suffered (Hebrews 5:8)

We now know through the life of Jesus Christ that faith is a mission from God, otherwise he would not have left heaven to come here. Christ was on a mission to obey the Father; therefore faith is an act of obedience or a mission to obey God. Obedience itself is a learned behavior, therefore if our savior had to learn it, then so will you. Faith or obedience comes by hearing God talk or by hearing the word of God. The word obey literally means to hear intelligently, or to act as if God himself is speaking. Now if obedience is the word of faith, then disobedience is the word of unbelief. Disobedience is what causes us to perish in our afflictions and die without knowledge of his deliverance. On the contrary, faith arrests our unbelief by denying us of our own discretion to depend upon his. Just so you know, obedience is the power to get wealth, causing us to rule, reign, and dominate in every situation that we face. However, disobedience will keep you out of victory lane and deny you access because of unbelief. Remember the children of Israel could not enter the Promised Land because of unbelief or the lack of confidence in God's righteous discretion and judgment. How do we achieve obedience? In the spirit realm you listen with your heart then out of the abundance of the heart the mouth will speak faith causing you to take action. Your heart must take pleasure in God's discretion before you can greatly delight in his commandments. Now when you listen for faith, you are actually listening for obedience because the power of God is in your obedience. Furthermore, the reason that you can hear obedience is because obedience is a spirit that enters your very soul. Jesus said my words they are spirit and they are life. So allow the word of God to penetrate your soul and launch you into your new destiny through your obedience.

Faith is now, faith has already experienced victory, and faith never struggles.

Day 17

Broken Vessels

And Jacob was left alone; and there wrestled a man with him until the breaking of the day. And when he saw that he prevailed not against him, he touched the hollow of his thigh; and the hollow of Jacob's thigh was out of joint, as he wrestled with him. (Genesis 32:24-25)

One of the greatest things that you can ever experience in life, is an encounter with God. An encounter is an unexpected meeting with God. When you have an encounter with God, you experience the fullness of joy because there is nothing broken, missing, and nothing else is needed. Imagine for a moment that your life is a container. Now all that stands between you and an encounter with God is a contaminated container called pride or the will of the flesh. An encounter occurs when the container is no longer able to keep its contents inside of the container because it has become broken. When a container becomes broken, whatever was inside will have an encounter with the outside. In other words the ingredients that is inside escape to the outside. Let me take this opportunity to let you know that all of hell is fighting you to make sure you don't humble yourself, lose your pride and become a broken vessel. Their job is to make sure that you don't surrender to God. They want to make sure that you stay in control of your own life, finances, future, and relationships. They want to ensure that your pride does not allow God free reign. However, whosoever exalteth himself shall be brought down, but he that humbleth himself shall be exalted, elevated or promoted. Satan is a good example of being brought down for he said "I will ascend into heaven, I will exalt my throne above the stars or angels of God". However Jesus described his downfall as a bolt of lightning fall from heaven. This is why the enemy wants you to continue to say just as Satan did "this is what I will do", while neglecting to make God first. Always keep in mind that the will of the flesh is the cage of the soul, but God is interested in the contents inside. Your soul is so precious that God would not even spare his own Son in exchange for your valuable contents. Instead, He sent his Son to lead our captivity captive, so that what is inside the cage would become broken. God's love was manifested through his Son so that we would be free to reign with Him.

Faith is actually God talk or talking on the God level, for without it you cannot communicate with him.

Day 18

Concentrate on the Blessing

Finally, brethren, whatsoever things are true, whatsoever things are honest, whatsoever things are just, whatsoever things are pure, whatsoever things are lovely, whatsoever things are of good report; if there be any virtue, and if there be any praise, think on these things (Philippians 4:8)

I'm here today to persuade you to concentrate on the blessing that God has spoken over your life, instead of concentrating on what is going on in your life. Remember that a blessing is simply a word or promise from God spoken in the spirit that manifests itself in the natural. In most cases you're either concentrating on the blessing or the effects of the curse. So don't pray for the blessing, and then choose the curse. Don't become like Esau who sold his birthright in exchange for temporary food to ease hunger pains.

> *Genesis 25:32: And Esau said, Behold, I am at the point to die, and what profit shall this birthright do to me. And Jacob said, Swear to me this day; and he swore unto him: and he sold his birthright unto Jacob.*

How many times does it seem that we can go no further: so we give in to the pain, the pressure, and depression of our emotions. Don't sell your birthright, for you have a right to prosperity, healing, deliverance, joy, happiness and peace. You have a right to these things that Jesus died to give you. There will always be repercussions when you trade in your birthright for pain. We can see here that Esau was not concentrating on his blessing, but concentrating on his need. He was weary and almost faint, but that is no excuse. His birthright afforded him the luxury of asking for what he needed from Jacob and he would have received the food for free. One of the greatest problems for God's people is recognizing the power and potential of your blessing when they are in need and under pressure. Remember the will of the flesh caters to the effects of our suffering, while the will of the spirit caters to our faith. Let us not forget that the Bible declares that we have all spiritual blessings necessary for our deliverance, if we will just concentrate on the blessing!

Faith is operated by the knowledge of God's love.

Day 19

Concentrate on the Blessing 2

But the children struggled together within her; and she said, "If all is well, why am I like this?" So she went to inquire of the LORD. And the LORD said to her: "Two nations are in your womb, two peoples shall be separated from your body; One people shall be stronger than the other, And the older shall serve the younger." (Genesis 25:22-23 (NKJV)

Notice again that there is a struggle over the blessing. Even today there are two sources of power in your life. A source of blessing and a source of cursing. One will produce the word of God causing manifestations of life. The other will produce a word from your flesh causing manifestations of death, depression, and destruction. Again, I repeat that your blessing involves a power struggle. Your blessing tells you who you are, what you have, and what you can do.

Genesis 32:24: And Jacob was left alone; and there wrestled a man with him until the breaking of the day.

Genesis 32: 27-28: And he said unto him, What is thy name? And he said, Jacob. And he said, Thy name shall be called no more Jacob, but Israel: for as a prince hast thou power with God and with men, and hast prevailed.

So most of the time when you have to wrestle for a blessing, it will require a name change. Here Jacob wrestles for the blessing, and you guessed it, he gets a name change. Now Jacob didn't see it coming, but his desire made him fight for something that he wanted. Always remember that you can have whatever blessings are in the will of God now, because he has already blessed you with them; you simply have to know how the blessings work and release them. Every good and perfect gift comes from above out of heavenly places. And since your blessing comes from above this makes your blessing a spiritual thing. So the thing that you are seeking God in the natural is a spiritual blessing that he has already given to you. Everything you see is something produced by spiritual power: so if a blessing is simply spiritual power from God, then this thing that I seek from God is produced by spiritual power that I already have. What this really means is that we should then concentrate on spiritual power because everything that you see is the product of something spiritual. Finally, concentrate on the blessing because it gives us power over the things that are not seen to do what we have been commissioned to do. Then we can receive what he wants us to have, and be what he wants us to be.

Faith is the outspoken expression of love in your heart toward God.

Day 20

Concentrate on the Blessing 3

Blessed be the God and Father of our Lord Jesus Christ, who hath blessed us with all spiritual blessings in heavenly places in Christ (Ephesians 1:3).

It is important to realize that God has given us his divine power which is activated through the knowledge of his love. That means that you are in charge of releasing the blessings. Now those blessings are in heavenly places so in order to release them you have to go where they are. It is important to observe that God, the Father of our Lord Jesus Christ is a spirit, and since we have been made in his image that makes us spirit beings also. Now what this really means is that we now have the power to transcend and go beyond the physical without ever leaving our bodies. So we can visit or even live in the past, enjoy the present, or live in the future. Did you ever have a conversation with someone in the present, but all of the time you could tell their heart or mind was not with you? Did it seem like they were somewhere else? Many times they are either entertaining their past hurts or failures, the insecurities of the present, or visiting the pain, stress and worry of the future. Please understand that you were made to feel or experience whatever you are thinking. For as a man is thinking in his heart, that is who he is! We have been trained to think bad thoughts if we sense that we are experiencing something bad. However, if we sense that we are experiencing something good, we think good thoughts. If these things are indeed true, then thinking is spiritual. This is a very common and overlooked fact by religious and even church people. We put more value on some of our other spiritual experiences not realizing that it is our everyday thinking that gives us the potential to experience heaven or hell on earth. Now our thinking is the product of spiritual thoughts whether good or bad that we have on any given subject. Then our thoughts hire or employ words to release into the natural what we have experienced in the spirit. Your success is depending upon what you are saying within yourself, because what you are saying within yourself is spiritual. Remember, you will never be more spiritual than what you are thinking.

Faith is your response to his love and sacrifice.

Day 21

Exercise Your Faith

For they verily for a few days chastened us after their own pleasure; but he for our profit, that we might be partakers of his holiness (Hebrews 12:10).

As we grow in the knowledge of our Lord and savior Jesus Christ, it is important to understand that he wants us to be partakers of his holiness or divine nature. It is for this reason that he allows us to encounter certain trials which are strictly for our profit. God wants us to exercise our faith and lean on the strength and power of the new man. So at some time during our trials he wants us to come to the conclusion that we will always be faced with two things which arc problems and promises. God wants our senses to become so sharp and trained, that whenever we are faced with a problem, test, trial, affliction, or challenge that we will always stand on the promises. Now this takes eating the right kind of spiritual food or a steady diet of the word of God which will produce faith. Faith is your response to what God has said, or simply standing on the promises. Faith is unquestioning belief that does not require further proof or evidence. Faith is the evidence itself of those things which we are hoping for. Now in order for faith to work properly it needs exercise. Exercise means to do something over and over until what you desire is accomplished. Therefore, spiritual exercise is simply to continue engaging in a test or trial with the same approach without focusing on the problems, but standing on the promises. Spiritual exercise is being diligent and becoming disciplined in your resolve. It is knowing that there is no other reliable or safe alternative but to trust God and stand on his promises. This will cause you to produce a harvest of fruit that consists of righteousness. The ability to think like, talk like and acting like God. When we think, talk, and act like God, we will get the same results that He gets when he approaches problems, stands and proclaims his own promise.

When you cash your check they give you the exact amount for which it is written, even so faith is the exact match for your need.

Day 22

Exercise Your Faith 2

But ye, beloved, building up yourselves on your most holy faith, praying in the Holy Ghost (Jude 1:20).

Like any other regiment, faith needs exercise in order to build itself up. Now in order for faith to build itself up it needs two things; it needs your problems and God's promises. The Bible is full of promises; but just in case you don't have enough problems, see if your neighbor has some extra ones. If you want to achieve success in the spiritual realm, exercising your faith is not optional. The Apostle Paul commanded the Philippian Church to work out and not to be lazy. That means to work out your own salvation with fear and trembling. One might ask why is it so important to exercise your faith? Well, everything that you need and desire from God is time sensitive. Mainly because to everything there is a season, and a time to every purpose under the heaven. God knows what we need, when we need it, and where it is coming from. He even has resources that we have not yet even considered. However, if we do not exercise our faith and workout to get into shape, it will be hard to believe when it is time to pray. So start lifting up your hands that are hanging down by faith, and begin calling those things which are not as though they were. Continue praying without ceasing, and remember that everything that you need now is manifesting now! Everything that has been manifesting is manifesting now. That which is to be manifested, has already been prearranged. God is just requiring that which is in him to be already past! In essence God is doing whatever you are praying in his will right now.

Faith is not a function of the human spirit, but an anointing to ask and believe.

Day 23

Independent Blessings

And I will make them and the places round about my hill a blessing; and I will cause the shower to come down in his season; there shall be showers of blessing (Ezekiel 34:26).

If we ever learn how to walk and chew bubblegum at the same time, then we will finally understand that God works independently of our senses. Many times your feelings and emotions lie by convincing you that your physical experience is greater than the one that you can or may not feel. So as you walk in the spirit, not only will you not carry out the thoughts and actions of the flesh, you will not depend on them either. Greater is the heavenly experience that is taking place in you than the one that you are experiencing with your natural senses in the world. Keep in mind that whatever thoughts are born of God will overcome the thoughts and the will of the flesh in the world. Godly affections will overcome earthly affections, and reveal what you love the most. So set your affections on things that are above and not on the things of the earth. Remember that your affections are reflections of your faith. Come boldly before the throne of grace to receive thoughts of mercy and grace. Watch your thoughts for they become words. Watch your words they become actions. Watch your habits they become character. Keep an eye on your character, for it is responsible for blessings. Now it is the will of God for you to have heaven on earth. So pray thy will be done in earth as it is in heaven. Rest with assurance that since it is his will, you can freely declare that you are experiencing what you are praying. For God has given you your heart's desire and has not withheld the request of your lips. Remember that whenever you are speaking God's word in faith, then God is speaking. Whenever God is speaking blessings are falling. Faith is the proof of unseen blessings, power and deliverance. So please keep in mind that blessings are timeless, for they were all made with God's spiritual authority and power.

Faith is simply taking advantage of every opportunity to speak God's word into the atmosphere against the challenges of your life.

Day 24

The Power of Words

And a certain centurion's servant, who was dear unto him, was sick, and ready to die (Luke 7:2).
Wherefore neither thought I myself worthy to come unto thee: but say in a word, and my servant shall be healed (Luke 7:7).

There is something that you should know. You have been trained to think bad thoughts based on what you are experiencing. However, you should always concentrate on blessings, because you were made to feel whatever you are thinking. Concentrating on blessings gives you power to think like God and dominate the unseen. The centurion's faith was released because he understood how authority works; he understood the power of words. The power of death and life is in the tongue, and you will eat the fruit of whatever you love by what you say. Words have meanings and paint their pictures into our lives. Your words are the transportation for your faith. So make sure that you are saying what you want to take place. Words give you the power to dominate the unseen. So remember that the things that are seen are not made of things which are appearing. This means that a blessing is a word from God concerning the unseen. No good thing will he withhold from them that walk uprightly, so make sure you are not staggering with doubt. Doubt will always manifest itself in what you say, because out of the abundance of the heart the mouth will speak. We should be more like Abraham who staggered not at the promise of God in unbelief, but was strong in faith, giving glory to God by what he said. Abraham was fully persuaded that what God had promised, he was able also to perform. Always keep in mind that to be strong in the faith means that you are concentrating on the blessing and ignoring the effects of the curse. Being strong in the faith means that you are ignoring circumstances and speaking life over dead things. Faith gives you the power of binding and loosing. It gives you power to release the unseen or keep something from operating. By your words you will be justified, and it is by your words that you attract condemnation.

Faith is in the unseen power of God, and victory in advance before the battle is even fought.

Day 25

Recognizing Victory

For whatsoever is born of God overcometh the world: and this is the victory that overcometh the world, even our faith (1 John 5:4).

When we talk about victory, it is defined as final and complete supremacy or superiority in battle or war. Victory does not occur when the battle is over, victory occurs when you know that the battle is won. It is also success in any contest or struggle involving the defeat of an opponent or the overcoming of obstacles. Now in this scripture God told the Apostle John to call the church together and introduce them to somebody who would make sure that the body of Christ was always rejoicing in triumph, no matter what trial that they faced. So John called on faith to come to encourage the saints and to give them confidence. With faith standing by, John said, "Allow me to present to some and introduce to others, God's warrior whom He calls the victory." This is the victory! This is the victory for your marriage. This is the victory for your finances. This is the victory for your health, and this is the victory for your home. Now faith does not appear to be victory until it reaches its full potential. Faith does not appear to be victory until it becomes exercised. It starts by building yourselves up on your most holy faith, praying in the Holy Ghost. Then you must change your diet from milk to meat. For every one who is no longer a child that continues to use milk is proving that they are still babes in Christ.

Those who are babes are unskillful in speaking the word of faith into their circumstances, also unskillful in prayer and making confessions. But strong meat belongs to them that are of full age, even those who by reason of use have their senses exercised to discern both good and evil. Remember faith needs exercise in order to build itself up. You should also keep in mind that you need both problems and promises so that your faith will have something meaningful to do. Therefore, my beloved brethren, be steadfast, unmovable, always abounding in the work of the Lord, forasmuch as ye know that your labor is not in vain in the Lord.

Faith is the victory that overcomes the world because faith is victory.

Day 26

Kingdom Living

Whereby are given unto us exceeding great and precious promises: that by these ye might be partakers of the divine nature, having escaped the corruption that is in the world through lust (2 Peter 1:4).

Our God is a matchless God who has made us complete in him. So he gets no pleasure out of us being sick, broke, depressed, or disgusted. Mainly because he has given us power to overcome all of these things. The eyes of the LORD are upon the righteous, and his ears are open unto their cry. However, God is looking for something specific so that he can manifest his power and do what he said. What we must do is to educate ourselves in kingdom living because God gets pleasure out of fulfilling his promises. Please keep in mind that He wants you to know exactly what it is that he requires. First of all, it is the will of God for you to receive your harvest. The work of God consists of planting his word and expecting a harvest. Now the harvest is everything that you ask God for in prayer while believing that you receive it. So you must learn how to pray without ceasing, meditate on his promises, and give yourself wholly to them. It is then that the Bible says that your profiting will appear unto all, for it is the Father's good pleasure to give you the kingdom. Remember that prayer and meditation produce the manifestation of the spirit that God has given to us, that we may profit from every trial, test, or challenge. The Greatest enemy of prayer is the ignorance of what it will do. For all things that you ask in prayer believing, you shall receive. Prayer is then the package that your faith comes in, for faith arrives and comes to God through prayer. In most cases it's not our lack of faith; it's our use of faith that keeps us from receiving what God has for us. Now God is always searching the hearts of men looking for the mind of the spirit, because the spirit of God has been assigned to making intercession for us. Therefore he always prays in oneness with the will of God. So praying in and with the spirit of God is truly kingdom living, because it allows God the freedom to take care of all of his citizens according to his will.

Faith is unique in that it has nothing to do with the natural.

Day 27

Kingdom Living 2

But seek ye first the kingdom of God, and his righteousness; and all these things shall be added unto you (Matthew 6:33).

Every day we choose whose kingdom we will live in and which power we will tap into. You will either operate in the kingdom of God, or tap into Satan's deception. If you are going to choose God's power then you must obey him. However, you will never be able to obey God until you believe him. Our challenge lies in renewing our minds and retraining it not to depend on the sense realm, and to operate independently of our feelings. If you are going to succeed in the kingdom, you must be well aware of how the laws of the kingdom work. Just because you receive him does not guarantee you success. Receiving his spirit only gives you the right to sonship. However, the power to experience sonship manifests itself in the ability to ask for what you want and need. God calls this ability prayer. Now there is no time in the spirit; meaning that whatever you ask God for is received instantly. That's why it is called kingdom living. Now God has chosen the right time for our breakthrough. A breakthrough is something that has to exist in one realm and penetrate the other with blessing. That blessing is simply a word from God in the spirit that penetrates the earth realm manifesting itself in the natural. Therefore, we must value the word because it is our blessing. This is one of the reasons that we must not put value in a form of godliness while denying the power of prayer its ability to work. Prayer always works! Your job is to decide by the power of prayer or the power of asking when your blessing will show up in heaven. God decides when it will show up in the earth.

> *Faith is made up of supernatural words that we use to describe what we see in the spirit.*

Day 28

Show Up

Thy kingdom come. Thy will be done in earth, as it is in heaven (Matthew 6:10).

Today God is essentially saying when you show me what you need from me in heaven through prayer, I will make it show up in the earth. In other words when his will shows up in heaven through you, it will show up in the earth for you. Another way of saying this is to set your affections on sending your treasure above to the kingdom realm, in preparation for a breakthrough in the natural realm. Seek to achieve your goals by not looking at the things that are seen. This achievement of success comes while looking at the things that are not seen. God's word warns us not to spend our time trying to lay hold on our treasures through the world's system. God doesn't want us to get caught up in manifestations but to spend our time walking in the spirit. Remember his goal is to reveal his glory in our lives. Now whoever you believe and whatever you believe is the object of your worship. We worship God by maintaining his spirit in our trials and tests while celebrating the truth. So seek the kingdom system instead, because God wants us to take care of our business from the place where he resides on the inside. If we delight ourselves in the spiritual part of our blessing, then God will give us the desires of our hearts in the natural.

It is the building material of those who believe for the supernatural.

Day 29

Faith to Believe

And suddenly there came a sound from heaven as of a rushing mighty wind, and it filled all the house where they were sitting (Acts 2:2).

On the Jewish Holiday called the day of Pentecost a special sound came from heaven. A sound is a noise with meaning. It is something that orders, indicates or proclaims a message while announcing where it has come from. Now when this sound came from heaven it was announcing the entrance and presence of the Holy Ghost with a signal requiring worship. In the natural, sound comes through your ears and then your mind tells your ears what you have heard. However, in the realm of the spirit sound comes through your spiritual ears then your spirit tells your spiritual ears what you have heard. Whenever a sound comes from heaven it is a rumor spread by the Holy Ghost about what you should believe. Therefore to believe means to respond to what you have heard in faith. The fact of the matter is that you cannot believe or respond to what you have not heard. So it makes sense that you cannot speak in a language that you have never heard. The wonderful thing about a word from God is that it comes not only with instructions, but the supernatural power to carry it out. This is called faith to believe. It is not some function of the human mind, but an anointing to trust God. So when this sound came, they were all filled with this faith to believe that they could speak in languages they had never learned. Then as they opened their mouths the manifestations of what they had believed became reality. The sound they heard from heaven was actually the Holy Spirit telling them to repeat after Him. Then they all began to speak with other tongues as the Spirit gave them the utterance. Faith to believe is exactly what we need in today's times. If you will listen closely, you will find that God is speaking to the mountains in our lives. He is opening closed doors, and discussing ways to escape. All he wants is for us to repeat what he is saying in the spirit, and we will see that it works in the natural.

Faith is the kingdom conversation of believers or a kingdom conversation with the king.

Day 30

Finish Your Work

And whatsoever ye do, do it heartily, as to the Lord, and not unto men. Knowing that of the Lord ye shall receive the reward of the inheritance: for ye serve the Lord Christ (Colossians 3:23-24).

As Christians, we have the hope of a better life, an abundant life through our inheritance which has been passed down through our spiritual family. The benefits of our inheritance are all inclusive, according as his divine power has given us all things pertaining both to life and godliness. This includes divine health, healing, financial independence, and prosperity of soul and mind. Our inheritance also includes freedom and liberty from all bondages, and even the blessings of salvation for our family, friends and neighbors. However, if you are going to come into your inheritance, you have to come out of unbelief. Having therefore these promises, let us cleanse ourselves from all filthiness of the flesh and spirit, perfecting holiness in the fear of God. Now unbelief is the filthiness of the flesh and spirit, and if you want to rid yourself of unbelief it takes work. Remember that the promises of God are inherited through the work of faith and patience. This requires diligence in the word of God and it also requires that you be not slothful in your work of believing. So ask yourself, did you work today? Did you work hard, or were you hardly working? Please know that God has provided a way of escape from the corruption of the world through his promises, but faith is the result of work or putting yourself in a position to hear his word. Remember, every test has its work. So if you don't work then you don't eat. If you don't eat, then you won't believe. Finally if you don't believe you won't receive the promises. Remember that believing is the work of faith, and the true test of faith is thanksgiving.

Faith is our way of asking God for the things that he bled and died to give us.

Day 31

Finish Your Work 2

For the Son of man is as a man taking a far journey, who left his house, and gave authority to his servants, and to every man his work, and commanded the porter to watch (Mark 13:34).

When Jesus went back to heaven the first thing that he did was give us power and authority over our trials. Upon receiving the Holy Ghost, delegated power was to be his first promise.

So God has given us three things with every test, trial, and temptation. He has given us authority over the trial, work in the trial, and instructions for the trial. Now since we have been endowed with this power from on high, the power over the trial is clearly not in the hands of Satan; it is in yours. Satan is not reigning in power or dominion over your trial, you are!

You see God has raised us up and made us to sit together in heavenly places of authority. Far above all principality, and power, and might, and dominion, and every name that is named, not only in this world, but also in that which is to come. This means that you cannot be tempted, tested, or tried by anything that is above what you are capable of overcoming. Anything that is above your capacity to dominate has been assigned to God himself andthe angels. This territory is considered his space. But of course his space is our space. Although he has given us authority over the trial, there is still work to do in the trial. This is the work of God that ye believe on him whom he hath sent. When he seated us with him in heavenly places he glorified us, but when we go to work in our trials, we glorify him. Now the power or authority that God has given you over your trial is present and ready to deliver you out of your captivity. The question is what are you going to do with it? What does having this power and authority really mean? Webster defines authority as the power or right to give commands, enforce obedience, take action or make final decisions. Jesus said that this power is the right to bind and to loose, to rule, reign and dominate.

It's time to go to work in the trial that you are facing at this very moment, and make sure you finish your work.

> *It is the way of access given by God to ask him for the things that are freely ours.*

Day 32

Using Your Authority

For I am a man under authority, having soldiers under me: and I say to this man, Go, and he goeth; and to another, Come, and he cometh; and to my servant, Do this, and he doeth it (Matthew 8:9).

Have you ever noticed how people in government exercise power to enforce laws?

Their power or influence comes from knowledge; in other words one needs to understand authority in order to use it effectively. In this lesson the Centurion said that he understood because he was under authority. The moral of this is that if you are not under it, you cannot understand it. If you have never been completely submitted, you will never completely understand why Satan must be completely submitted to you. The Centurion said when you are under authority and have others who are submitted to you, that you can say come and they will come, or go and they will go. He then said, because of this I also understand the spirit realm. You don't have to come where I am, just speak the word! What an amazing display of faith and believing. So what does it take to believe? First of all you have to become a hearer of the word with your spiritual ears, and proceed to becoming a doer of what you just heard. A doer responds to the word with work because the word gives vision of change. So a doer responds to the word, but you cannot respond to what you cannot hear. Hearing takes work. So be advised that God will not give more vision of liberty and change than what you are willing to work for. When can we say of a truth that we believe the promises of God that have been made available to us? The answer is when it gets into our hearts. Remember that the true sign that the word has gotten into our hearts is when we are able to declare the promise in power and at will!

It is the language of the Holy Spirit or the language of the kingdom.

Day 33

The Power Plant

For the Son of man is as a man taking a far journey, who left his house, and gave authority to his servants, and to every man his work, and commanded the porter to watch (Mark 13:34).

When we receive Jesus as our savior he gives us power to overcome all of our tests and trials by manufacturing faith in our lives. Our lives become mini power plants of his corporation.

Jesus is like an employer whose plant or business is a manufacturing plant in our trial. The plant manufactures faith. Just imagine with me that he had to go on a business trip for his father so hc makes plans to leave the business in good hands. Imagine that he gave authority to his faithful employees. To every man he gave a particular job, work to do, and let them know that he would be back sometime soon. The job that he gave was to walk by faith, to believe his promises, and believe for provision in every trial. Now even though his employees know that he is returning to the plant, will he find that they have manufactured the faith to continue running the business? In the meantime the thief shows up to break into the plant trying to steal kill and destroy any possible faith that you have manufactured in your trial. Now our employer has hired security to watch over us while we are hard at work. Yet we are so easily moved and frustrated when things go wrong, mainly because it seems that we can do nothing about our building being broken into. However, we must keep in mind that the employer knows what is going on. You see he has installed security cameras with the technology to send the images to his phone. He knows exactly what is going on but wants to see how we are going to react. This reminds me of Mary and Martha when Lazarus their brother was sick. Again we see how Jesus went on a business trip for his Father and left Mary, Martha and Lazarus to run the business while he was gone; but soon after, word came that Lazarus had called in sick and that the production there was slowing down. However, Jesus did not panic or worry for he knew that even though there was a slowdown in the plant, that it would produce more than it ever did before. So he remained where he was until the word came that the plant had been shut down because Lazarus was dead. Then Jesus told his partners that were with him on the trip, that now it is time to go and check on the plant. Now when he got there he found the plant closed, the product sitting around, and the employee morale low. Martha who was one of the supervisors, said "Jesus if you had been here in spite of this situation we could have kept the plant open for business"; But then Jesus shocked her and said that the plant is open and running right now. We are producing something new. A plant that works when you are not in the plant, this particular plant is in you. It's called a power plant. It doesn't work by your might, or your own power, but by God's spirit says the Lord. Before I left you I planted a new microchip in your heart that began production when you would be too weak to continue your work. You see whenever you get weak, that's when the power plant begins to work. So when you are weakest, that's when you are the strongest.

Faith is the evidence that believers look for who are speaking his language and acting on God's word.

Day 34

Heaven on Earth

And when he was demanded of the Pharisees, when the kingdom of God should come, he answered them and said, The kingdom of God cometh not with observation:. Neither shall they say, Lo here! or, lo there! for, behold, the kingdom of God is within you (Luke 17:20-21).

There is a place where God the Father and the Son sit on thrones surrounded by angelic hosts. It is the place where the souls of them who have departed and died in the faith reside. The streets there are paved with pure gold, the gates made of pearls, and the scriptures tell of a sea of glass like crystal. It is the place that we call heaven. However there is another place that is within you called the kingdom of God, or heaven on earth. Heaven on earth is a state of mind in the Lord produced by the righteousness, peace and joy of the Holy Ghost. It is experienced when the mind leaves the confines of our natural body and its senses to visit heavenly places that are embedded even deeper within us. Heaven on earth is not experienced by the power of the mind in and of itself, but by the spirit of the Lord. The Spirit of God is what takes our natural mind to the kingdom of God. That's why the Bible said "let this mind be in you which was also in Christ Jesus". It is the heavenly mind enabling our natural mind to experience heaven on earth. Yes, the kingdom of God or Heaven on earth is within you. Now neither flesh and blood, nor the will of the flesh is able to enter the kingdom that contains these blessings. However, his divine power has enabled our minds through his spirit to leave the physical realm and go where the blessings are. We are instructed by the word to grab or lay hold on eternal life by laying hold on the blessings. Mainly because the kingdom of God is overflowing with blessings waiting to be released in the earth. You are responsible and in charge of releasing your own blessings. The way that you achieve this is to believe that you are receiving as you pray. Now the scriptures declare that God has given us all spiritual blessings in heavenly places. This means that we must go where they are to release them. These blessings that are in heavenly places are not there in the form of cars, homes, money, or jobs. You see there is nothing natural in the spiritual realm. What we call blessings in the natural are simply the thoughts and plans of God employed by his word to bring them to pass. Think of God as the master architect who has drawn up wonderful plans for your life, & contracted his word to frame what he has been thinking. God has given us the divine power of prayer to lay hold on these spiritual blessings and bring them into the natural. In other words heaven on earth is accomplished by believing that you are experiencing what you are praying, at the time that you are praying for it. The fact of the matter is that your faith believes that you are experiencing what you desire when you pray. Notice that when Jesus spoke to the fig tree that nothing seemed to happen. However, as they passed by the next day, they noticed that the fig tree had dried up from the roots. Their conclusion was that the fig tree was experiencing what He said, when He said it.

Faith is a demonstration of God's attributes.

Day 35

Moving Without the Ball

A land which the LORD thy God careth for: the eyes of the LORD thy God are always upon it, from the beginning of the year even unto the end of the year (Deuteronomy 11:12).

There is a place that God has been trying to get us to all year. It is a place of health, financial independence, and kingdom living. However, in order for us to get there, God has to change the way we think about his instructions. The way you think about his instructions are responsible for the place you are in life at this very moment. When you follow his instructions you can rest assured that God has something in his hands that is about to show up in yours. Imagine with me that you have a basketball goal in your backyard and you are waiting to play. The Basketball goal represents a change in your thinking. Imagine also that God has chosen you to be on his team. His purpose for choosing you is to bring forth fruit from his word. He has ordained you, meaning that he has given you a mission with him called a commission. Now every commission is an agreement between two parties or a contract. The Bible is that contract. If you will look closely at the document, you will notice that God has given us a large contract based on what we do regarding fruit or souls. He even said, "If we will ask any thing in his name, He will do it." Now in a basketball game the enemy or challenger is always taken by surprise when the ball shows up in the hands of the opposition and they didn't see it coming. The result is always easy points that contribute to the victory. The trick is learning how to move without the ball. The person moving without the ball is not surprised when the ball shows up unannounced because it is a designed play. The ball is supposed to be there! So it is with God; those on his team have to show up at the goal in faith without the manifestation, knowing that it is a designed play and what he promised will be there! Now let me tell you about some of the things that drive a coach crazy. Standing around waiting for the ball so you can take a shot is not walking by faith. You should be moving without the ball and letting it come to you. By now I hope you realize that I am talking about the kingdom and how to play in this game of eternal life. We should be going where the sinners are and expecting our needs to be met as we go. Moving without the ball is simply walking by faith, and not by sight.

Faith activates the power of God and gives him permission to act on your behalf.

Day 36

No Excuses, Shoot the Ball

And they all with one consent began to make excuse. The first said unto him, I have bought a piece of ground, and I must needs go and see it: I pray thee have me excused. And another said, I have bought five yoke of oxen, and I go to prove them: I pray thee have me excused. And another said, I have married a wife, and therefore I cannot come (Luke 14:18-20).

Have you noticed that people have all kind of excuses for not doing what God saved them for? They use everything from blaming it on their jobs, families, lack, sickness, to abuse or whatever else has happened to them. One day the disciples were complaining about what they were giving up for him. And Jesus answered and said, Verily I say unto you, There is no man that hath left house, or brethren, or sisters, or father, or mother, or wife, or children, or lands, for my sake, and the gospel's, but he shall receive an hundredfold now in this time, houses, and brethren, and sisters, and mothers, and children, and lands, with persecutions; and in the world to come eternal life. What if Jesus had said this cross is too heavy, beam me up! Jesus said unto his disciples, if any man will come after me, let him deny himself, and take up his cross, and follow me. Again, when you sacrifice your life for his sake and the Gospels', we call that moving without the ball. God wants you to always be ready to dunk the ball, or score for the kingdom. Now you cannot show up in faith to be where you are supposed to be for the dunk shot without hearing the word. In this game of eternal life the goal is to get people saved and filled with His spirit! Getting people saved and filled is a 3 pointer, and edifying the body is like a free throw. Whenever the players on the team are falling behind or not performing to expectations, the coach will call a time out for a designed play. Having church is the call to the side lines which we call a time out, and prayer is the designed play drawn up by the Father. Many times when the coach calls the team to the side lines, he has noticed that they are weary and realizes that it is time to renew their minds. He tells them to ignore the circumstances and uses words that we call a pep talk to get their minds stayed on him. So if you seem to be falling behind in life and don't like the score, call a time out. Changing your thinking changes your actions and getting God involved in your actions changes your situation.

Faith is the realm that celebrates what God has done today.

Day 37

Your Heart's Desire

Thou hast given him his heart's desire, and hast not withholden the request of his lips. Selah (Psalms 21:2).

I want to talk to you today about how to get your heart's desire from God and experience heaven on earth. Your heart's desire was made to be put into words, if not it will inflict pain and even cause sickness. It will give you the spirit of heaviness, make you double minded, and the organs of your body could shut down when you do not release your heart's desire. So your heart's desire should be your prayer to God. Now the natural and the spiritual realm are two different worlds. They work independently of each other, yet they both work together for our good. However, there are two facts that we deem important and that is you can have heaven on earth but you cannot have the earthly or the natural realm in heaven; because flesh and blood cannot possess the kingdom of God. This means that you must walk and live in the spirit to possess spiritual blessings, or what we call heaven on earth. What gets done in the spirit realm cannot be done with the aid of the natural realm. On the contrary, what

89

gets done in the natural cannot even exist without the aid of the spirit because the things that are seen are not made of things that do appear. Nothing really gets done without prayer, however if you do not know what God is doing while you are praying, then you are asking amiss. When you pray you maintain freedom; for where the spirit of prayer is there is also liberty. This is the secret to prayer, believing that you are experiencing the request as you pray. Prayer is no fun and unexciting unless you get what you pray for. It makes no sense unless you get what you ask for. Now God has given to every man a measure of faith and at the same time Satan offers every man a measure of doubt. If you feed your doubts your faith will play dead. However, if you feed your faith your doubts will starve to death. What you say within yourself is either your faith or your doubt talking. So consider what your doubt says concerning the things of God. Your doubt says when I see it I will believe it. Your faith says I don't need to see it to believe it because I myself am the evidence. You see your faith believes that you are experiencing what you desire, when you pray. Now if you have a desire that you want to see come to past then, there are some things that you need to pay attention to. Whenever you have a desire, pay attention to the promise, faith, and the manifestation. A promise is simply a talking word from God in the spirit realm. Whenever you actually hear a promise from God in the spirit realm then faith will come as the evidence to take the place of the promise. It is there because you heard, and hearing is seeing. Then, while faith is standing guard in your heart as the promise, manifestation will show up and send faith home for its next assignment. This is how you get your needs met, and your heart's desire.

Faith is having a kingdom mentality and providing a godly response to your problems and tests.

Day 38

Your Heart's Desire 2

*Delight thyself also in the LORD; and he shall give thee
the desires of thine heart (Psalm 37:4).*

Have you ever wondered how Abraham was able to
believe God without doubting or staggering? How did he
get to the place of being fully persuaded that what God
had promised he was able also to perform? He simply got
over into the realm where God is. He got into the realm
where God is unhindered by doubt and unbelief.
Abraham was able to do this because he spent time in
the spirit realm; he spent time with God in prayer. Now
prayer is simply confirmation of your agreement with
God. Believing takes work; but that work is just a matter
of getting in position to believe. However, you cannot be
lazy; you have to go to work! You are experiencing right
now whatever you are believing. This is the secret to
prayer believing that you are experiencing your request
independently of your feelings as you pray. As we pray
we are changed into the same image that we see, the key
word being (into). In other words, whatever you focus on
is what you are into, and whatever you are into is into

you. If you focus on deliverance and victory they will have a divine effect on you. They will change you into one who has been delivered and one who has experienced victory. One of the laws of the spirit says that whatever you are seeing is what you are thinking, and whatever it is that you are seeing is what will be seen in you. This is the confidence that we have in him, if we know that he is listening to us. If we are really cognizant of Him listening, then we know that we have the petitions that we desired of him. The law of Sonship declares that he freely gives us all things. So if you don't know what God is doing while you are praying then you are missing an opportunity for manifestations. Now the peace of God gives us a clue of how things work in the spiritual realm, which is simply past our understanding. In other words, we don't need to understand how! In the natural when we see, feel, hear, smell or touch we understand. However, when we pray in the spirit and believe, it bypasses our senses and causes our spiritual understanding to open its eyes. We open our eyes when we hear his word, which are the eyes of our understanding. The eyes of our understanding become enlightened. To enlighten means to give the light of fact and knowledge; to reveal truths free from ignorance; to give clarification of meanings and intentions; or to have the heart flooded with light. When we believe we see what he said, and when we believe what he said we see what we heard.

Faith is the realm of the now, and the switch that turns God's power on.

Day 39

Manifesting the Promises

That I may make it manifest, as I ought to speak (Colossians 4:4).

God is trying to develop us in the area where we are struggling with his word; so above all he wants us to know how to get manifestations into our lives. First of all, the manifestation of the Spirit is given to us to profit with in every situation. Therefore, he wants us to concentrate on the spiritual so that we get what we want in the natural. One of the greatest revelations that you can ever discover is this. If it manifests to you in the spirit, then it will manifest to you in the natural.

So we must begin to value spiritual things because whatever it is that you desire is spiritual. Everything is spiritual because no matter how big that it is, it still fits into your heart. Get it? Now God has already blessed us with all spiritual blessings in heavenly places in Christ. This includes everything that you can ever desire. So your first lesson in manifestations should be in declaring; I am experiencing the spiritual blessing of my heart right now, because I am experiencing whatever I am thinking and praying. Now Father, I release every financial, healing, family, and relationship blessing available and unknown to me at this very moment. What you are praying is done whenever you know that he hears you, which is whenever you pray in his will. God will do what you pray when you pray, because it is he that is at work praying through you. This is true worship. Remember you experience what you worship and you worship what you see. The prayer of faith is the key to manifestation, but worship is key to the actual experience before it manifests in the natural. This is important because what you think about, you experience. Now with that being said, praying the word is the key to experiencing whatever things that you desire. That's why Jesus said "whatever the things are that you desire, when you pray, believe that ye receive them, and ye shall have them. For when you experience what you desire, it brings joy to life and the fulfillment of heaven on earth.

Faith is based on what we know about the love of God.

Day 40

Manifesting the Promises 2

Whereby are given unto us exceeding great and precious promises: that by these ye might be partakers of the divine nature, having escaped the corruption that is in the world through lust. (2 Peter 1:4)

God has manifestation on his mind and has given us the manifestation of his spirit to profit with in every endeavor that we engage in for him. This will be an incredible season of power because both grace and peace are being multiplied for the kingdoms sake. God wants there to be a noticeable difference between the world and His children, therefore he has given us exceeding great and precious promises. These promises have been designed to take us from the bottom to the top. They will bring us from the back to the front of the line. We will view God's blessings from above and not beneath, simply because he has decided to make us the head and not the tail. It is by these promises that we become partakers of the divine nature and escape the debt, depression, sin and sickness, while defeating our every enemy. Now these promises are designed to provide an escape from falling in love with money and keep us in love with God. The love of money is still the root of all evil, because if the people of God did for Him what they do for money, we would understand what it means to be in oneness with God. You can always tell who a person is in love with by who they spend their time with. Determining who you have allegiance to is a simple test, because no man can serve two masters. If you love God you will give him your time, and if you are chasing money it will consume your time. You see our jobs were never designed to be our source, or to take us away from God. This delicate balance of having money and not allowing the chase to have us is what God originally had in mind. Please understand that it is not your job or your schedule, it is you that God is looking at through your heart. We are to cleanse ourselves from everything that contaminates our flesh or limits our faith to pursue perfect oneness with God. Now we have in our earthen vessels a treasure designed to demonstrate the excellence and the power of our God. It knows no boundaries, no fear, and no limits. It is able to do exceeding and abundantly above all that we can ask or think but only works according to the knowledge that is in us, even though we are as Kings and priests unto our God and are in love with Him. Regardless of the fact that we are a royal priesthood of the most high God. As sons and daughters of his majesty we must not allow our familiarity with our Father to sabotage our desire to know him even more.

> *Faith is spiritual genius because it calls things which be not as though they were, then adds corresponding actions that cause manifestations to take place.*

Day 41

Manifesting the Promises 3

My people are destroyed for lack of knowledge: because thou hast rejected knowledge, I will also reject thee, that thou shalt be no priest to me: seeing thou hast forgotten the law of thy God, I will also forget thy children (Hosea 4:6).

Many times as people of God we have rejected instructions, not realizing that instructions bring knowledge. You see, whatever it is that you desire but have not claimed in the spirit is simply a reflection of your lack of knowledge and how faith works. In most cases it has to do with what you don't know about prayer and manifestations. Knowledge is what attracts grace, favor, and peace. It is when we cry after knowledge, and lift up our voices for understanding; when we seek her like money and search for her as for hidden treasures. It is then that we will understand the wisdom of God and discover his knowledge. When we seek the Lord, we seek the manifestation of His Spirit that he has given us to profit with. In essence, when the spirit of God is manifested, we gain a greater knowledge of who he is. Our knowledge of Him changes either by a new trial, test, or by the extension of the one that we are in. Your trial will work something new in you and give you something that you did not have, which is a greater knowledge of who he is. That's why we count it all joy when we encounter new trials or when the one that we are in is extended. Now we realize that God has given us an invitation to the trial that we are in, so that we can gain a greater knowledge of who he is in the spirit. It is important to realize that the greatest times of manifestation will always come in times of weakness. So if you're wondering why God hasn't shown up in your trial, the answer is because he already has. God wants to make us sensitive in the natural to what he is doing and has done in the spirit. The trying of your faith exercises your senses to what God is doing over time. In fact, his strength is made perfect or comes to its full potential when we are the weakest. Furthermore, God will always manifest himself when he can get the glory.

Faith is a vision from God of you accomplishing your goal.

Day 42

Releasing Your Prosperity

If they obey and serve him, they shall spend their days in prosperity, and their years in pleasures. (Job 36:11)

The level of your prosperity is based upon your level of obedience. If you want to change your level of prosperity, your level of obedience has to change. Now in order to change your level of obedience, you must change your level of faith. Levels of faith are changed with every situation and circumstance that requires believing God without seeing your way out.

The righteousness of God or the release of your prosperity is revealed by your faith. Righteousness is what God does in response to his word. You see righteousness which is God's response to doers of his word, is revealed and made abundant by our faith. You see we go from faith to faith and glory to glory. When we are both willing and obedient to God's instructions, God promises to give us the blessings of our land. Now our quest for obedience of faith may be obtained quicker if we know what obedience is. Obedience is something that you hear in order to comply with. Though it seems to elude you, please understand that obedience is in your mouth and in your heart. Obedience is something heard in the spirit that causes us to move! Obedience is simply a sacrifice, the putting aside of something valued for the sake of something else having a more pressing claim. To obey means that I value God's opinion, his instruction and his discretion over my own.. We experience the supernatural life of prosperity by living and obeying every word. Now in order to change your level of faith you must change your level of love. So if you want to keep making steady progress in prosperity, you must keep yourself informed of God's love, while continuously looking for the mercy of our Lord through eternal life. Not only should we keep ourselves within the boundaries where God's love can reach us, but we should keep ourselves in love with him. We keep ourselves in love with him by encountering his presence, because once you encounter his presence you are never the same.

When you have faith you are simply laying claim to something that God has already provided which means that something that you were hoping for has now become yours.

Day 43

The Speed of Relationships

By faith Abraham, when he was called to go out into a place which he should after receive for an inheritance, obeyed; and he went out, not knowing whither he went. By faith he sojourned in the land of promise, as in a strange country, dwelling in tabernacles with Isaac and Jacob, the heirs with him of the same promise. (Hebrews 11:8-9)

Everything moves at the speed of relationships. Sara was able to have a child when she was beyond childbearing age because of Abraham's relationship with God. In addition both Isaac and Jacob became heirs of the same promise that God made with Abraham. So we can see that relationships are powerful when you make them with God. Another thing that we can see by this is that manifestations occur at the speed of obedience. Manifestations are supernatural processes; however, the speed of your manifestation or progress in life is based on the speed of godly inspired relationships. You are promoted in life at the speed of your relationships and how fast they escalate. So manifestations take place at the speed of your relationships. Everything in the natural is the result of a relationship with something in the spirit. The things that are seen are not made of things which do appear, because nothing just happens! Your promotion in the earth will take place because you have a relationship with somebody! God does not want us to think that everything is spiritual without a relationship to the natural. In the Bible a man by the name of Mordecai was promoted to 2nd in command in their kingdom because of his relationship with Esther. People had never heard of Bishop T.D. Jakes until he was promoted because of a relationship with Jan Crouch. We have our church building because of a relationship between my uncle and the top man in a local Catholic Diocese. It was because of a relationship which my uncle forged, that allowed me into the office of this important man in the Catholic Church. My uncle convinced this clergyman who managed thousands of properties to sell us this property for a fraction of its worth. That relationship enabled us to purchase this property without it ever hitting the market. My relationship with Roman Phifer, a 3 time super bowl champion, caused him to send a $90,000 check to my house for the down payment on our church. However, this transaction could only take place because of a divine relationship with my pastor, Bishop Steve Houpe. After planting a $1000 seed into our Bishop, God used him as an instrument to release a word of prosperity, abundance, and increase that came to pass, exactly like he said.

Faith is the voice of his word.

Day 44

The Speed of Relationships 2

And they said unto him, Where is Sarah thy wife? And he said, Behold, in the tent. And he said, I will certainly return unto thee according to the time of life; and, lo, Sarah thy wife shall have a son. And Sarah heard it in the tent door, which was behind him (Genesis 18:9-10).

The notion of what God says is going to take place is usually sheer foolishness, ridiculous, and hilarious to the natural man. Just ask Sarah, that's why she initially laughed at the idea and made fun of having a child at age 90. She jokingly said, "shall my Lord still have pleasure in the bedroom?". Through faith also Sara herself received strength to conceive seed, and was delivered of a child when she was past age, because she judged him faithful who had promised. Now notice that Sara participated in three things because of Abraham's faith. She received strength to conceive seed, was delivered when she was past age, and abundance showed up because she judged him faithful who had promised. Like Sara, when we believe and conceive, we cause life to begin in our spiritual womb. Our conception means to form or develop in the mind or spirit through the imagination. It means holding the word as our conviction and opinion. You will always do things differently when you become pregnant with the word. When you become pregnant it changes the way you do things. Now Sarah represents the Church of today. The Church is the Woman with the womb. This is why God uses his servants, especially those who are in the five fold ministry to plant seed into his woman. The word will produce fruit. Some people wonder why Worship is so important. Well worship is the foreplay that prepares the woman to receive the seed under the right conditions so that the seed is received with joy. The joy of the Lord is the strength to receive the seed. The joy that comes from foreplay or worship is the key to becoming pregnant with the word. Now just because you have sex does not mean that you become pregnant. However, once you become pregnant it changes the way that you do things. It changes the way that you think, dress, and act because you are being careful to protect the seed. So if you are pregnant with God's Word, protect the seed! Now it is really important to understand that God has chosen his word to bring about the plan and purpose that he has for your life. Nothing happens without the word, so say it! No peace, no joy, no prosperity, no manifestation; God does everything by his word! Now our relationship with God is exactly the same relationship that we have with his word. Why, because in the beginning was the Word, and the Word was with God, and the Word was God. The same was in the beginning with God. Now if the word was God, then the word is God. This means that however much we are reading, meditating, and fellowshipping with God's word, is a Kodak moment of our relationship with God right now. God is looking for somebody to take a picture with so that he can take that picture and show the world that they are together. He wants everybody to know that they have a relationship, and are in love. Everything good in the world is the result of its relationship with God. So every good and perfect gift comes from above and has the handprint, and signature of God on it. In light of this fact, one of the most important things that we can ever understand is that the speed of your progress in life is based on the speed of your relationships with God and with man. You are promoted in life at the speed of which you develop relationships, and the same is true about manifestations. So again we can see by this that manifestations occur at the speed of obedience. Now the first step to manifestations is to hear the word. Remember you can't hear if you are not here. Ask yourself if I don't get that Word does it hinder the progress of my manifestation? When God gave Abraham the word, Sara heard it because she was there listening in the tent behind them. Ask yourself if God sends a word to your church, is it for you? Ask yourself, "If I can't make it to church was that word for me?"

Faith is having an unquestioning belief that needs no further proof or evidence.

Day 45

How to Possess Your Vessel

That every one of you should know how to possess his vessel in sanctification and honour (1 Thessalonians 4:4).

Now, it is a common belief among Christians today that if people keep falling into sin that perhaps they are not born again. However, in many cases it's not that the people are not truly saved, but perhaps the problem is that they do not know how to yield to their new nature. In other words many of God's people do not know how to properly possess their vessel, and frankly speaking are unaware of their new superhero, the new creature.

God is able to keep you from falling, and to present you faultless before the presence of his glory with exceeding joy. However, if God is going to present you faultless, it cannot be based upon your works...you will somehow blow it again. God wants you to get past that through something called progressive sanctification. Please understand that being free from sin doesn't mean that you will never make another mistake, it just means that you are covered under His policy or covenant. This is not a license to sin, but God doesn't want you to fall into condemnation either. Sanctification is simply a license to live Holy.

The question many new converts and even seasoned saints alike are asking is this, "Although I believe that it is possible, how do I live a life free from sin?" The answer and formula for living free from sin is found in:

> *Romans 10:10: For with the heart man believeth unto righteousness; and with the mouth confession is made unto salvation.*
>
> *Genesis 15:6: And he believed in the LORD; and he counted it to him for righteousness.*

Living free from sin is something the Bible calls righteousness. It is with the heart that man believes unto righteousness, and this transaction is made complete with the confession of the mouth. Nothing that you do in and of itself that is without the spirit of God will ever be counted as righteousness. It can even be right, but that doesn't make it righteousness. God would have been right to send us all to hell because of Adam's sin, but his righteousness would not allow him to do it. Righteousness can only be achieved through the blood of Jesus. You can't achieve righteousness until you believe God for it. Trying to keep his commandments without faith in His blood will only lead to frustration. Now the key to this power is identity and the power to overcoming sin is in identifying with the blood.

Faith says about itself what it discovers about God, for as He is so are we.

Day 46

How to Possess Your Vessel 2

But God be thanked, that ye were the servants of sin, but ye have obeyed from the heart that form of doctrine which was delivered you. Being then made free from sin, ye became the servants of righteousness. In other words you were made free from sin by confessing and believing what the scripture says (Romans 6:17-18).

We must learn to make God our Sabbath or rest from this labor of trying to live holy, and being made righteous. You see there is a rest that remains available for the people of God through faith in the blood of Jesus, and what He did on Calvary. God is to be thanked that you were the servants of sin, but now the key is that you have obeyed from the heart. Being then made free from sin, you became the servants of righteousness. We have to get to a point in our lives that even though our minds don't understand it, we say what God is saying any way. Always remember that the natural man cannot receive the things of God, neither can he know them because they are spiritually discerned. Again we must remember that with the heart man believes to the point of righteousness, however, the transaction is not complete until you say it! So although you are made in the image of God nothing takes place until you say something. You must declare that you are free from sin. Keep in mind that before you believed to the point of righteousness you were a servant of sin. However, when you obeyed from the heart, righteousness stepped up and took over your labor. In addition, let us also not forget that righteousness is any action that satisfies the justice of God, therefore Jesus is our righteousness. His death is what satisfied requirements of a Holy God. So when it comes to works, or doing what is right, righteousness is not so much what you are doing, but what he has done instead. It is therefore imperative that you spend your day talking about who you are in him, mainly because you do it anyway, that is you are always talking to yourself. Lots of Christians go through their day saying, I'm sick, broke, depressed and hurting. Why not say that you are the righteousness of God, a vessel of his activity in the earth.

Faith can never be anything other than victory.

Day 47

How to Possess Your Vessel 3

For he hath made him to be sin for us, who knew no sin; that we might be made the righteousness of God in him (2 Corinthians 5:21).

When the blood of Jesus was applied to your life, you in fact became the righteousness of God. Yes, the blood caused you to become an image of his Son! Keep in mind that out of the abundance of the heart the mouth speaketh, and as a man thinketh in his heart so is he. (Proverbs 23:7) Your mind is turned off for very little time, so turn it off and think through your new creature which is engulfed with the mind of Christ. God wants you to know what you have and who you are in him. Remember that as batter is to chicken, and the chicken is to gravy, so we have been created in righteousness. For if any man be in Christ Jesus, he is a new creature. Old bondages and limitations have passed away, and behold all things are made new. Turn off the old man and put on the new man. Put on the new man by virtue of your faith and confession, which after God is created in righteousness and true holiness. We must also keep in mind that we are making a distinction between Salvation and Sanctification. Salvation is like the joy of a new car, but sanctification is the joy of a new car wash. So when it rains you don't have to buy a new car, you only have to wash it. This is what we call progressive sanctification. Jesus said, "Now are you clean through the word". This means that God has released you from all the bondage of sin and it's addictions through faith in His word. God wants us to know that we live, move and have the privilege of being in him. (Acts 17:28) This is referring to the new creature and just like a new car shines after being washed, so does your new creature. Everyone knows where they live and almost no-one goes to the wrong house. Therefore, it is imperative that we spend time at home in Christ. Paul said if we live in the spirit; let us also walk in the spirit confessing who we are in Christ. Salvation is settled so just because you are walking in the flesh or visiting the will of the flesh, does not mean that this is the place where you live. These blessings and benefits are however realized by those who walk not after the flesh, but after the spirit. Just keep in mind that you are walking where you are talking. Whenever you see someone who is defeated in their minds, you should automatically know what they have been telling themselves all that day. This is another reason that we speak to ourselves in psalms, hymns, and spiritual songs. Making melody in our hearts to the Lord should be our full time occupation, because we are telling ourselves something anyway. Instead of meditating on the fact that you messed up again, tell yourself that you are free from the bondage of sin and its addictions. Instead of concentrating on what you don't have, remind yourself that your God will supply all of my needs. He does not operate according to what you see, but according to his riches in glory which are unseen. (Phil. 4:19)

Faith works by love and love is always a process.

Day 48

How to Possess Your Vessel 4

Then said Jesus unto his disciples, If any man will come after me, let him deny himself, and take up his cross, and follow me. For whosoever will save his life shall lose it: and whosoever will lose his life for my sake shall find it. (Matthew 16:24-25)

If you are going to follow Jesus, you must take up your cross. This means that you must deny yourself of anything which is standing in the way of your obedience to God. Any time you sin it simply means that you decided to save your life. Consequently when you decide to save your own life you lose your life or fellowship with God. You must make a conscious decision to bear your cross or deny yourself of ungodly pleasures in order to stay in fellowship with God. Remember you must suffer in the flesh, just as Christ himself did. When you decide to suffer in the flesh it is then that you cease from sin. Therefore we must put our faith in God's ability to keep us, and don't take your life back! Put your faith in God's discretion concerning that thing, and let God keep you. Now if you really want to start experiencing the benefits of sanctification, then you need to make a commitment to sanctify yourself daily. Too many people have

119

stumbled into sin and then laid there unnecessarily, when all they had to do was get up and go to the car wash of the word. The scriptures declare that if we confess our sins that he is able and just to forgive us and cleanse us from all unrighteousness. Remember that dirt and mud mean nothing to God, for you are new in him everyday. All you need is the washing of the water by the word. This is why we should make righteousness our greatest treasure because it is kept in heavenly places where the dirt, mud and dust of sin will not corrupt. Sometimes it seems as if we are the only ones who are facing and caught up in the mess that we are in. However, it is important to note that all have sinned and come short of the glory of God. Furthermore, there is no good thing in the flesh. Jesus said there is none that is good in and of himself, none but the Father. Everyone has a cross and must take up his cross and follow Jesus. Remember, whosoever does not bear his cross, and come after Jesus, cannot be His disciple. Now the will of the flesh will always be called upon to die, so that the new creature can live freely in you. This is not a one shot deal and must be dealt with daily. Death through your cross is simply passing from one realm to another, and actually you are going from faith to faith. You are going from faith on this side of your trial to faith on the other side of your trial. Therefore, if you are going to successfully crucify the will of the flesh, you must have a valid reason for it to die. You must have something else to focus on other than the pain and agony of the present. Now what enabled Jesus to endure his cross was the joy that was set before him. The Bible tells us to look unto Jesus who is in charge of our transportation to the other side of our trial. There is joy on the other side, but you have to keep looking at Jesus in order to get it. Sometimes it is hard to find joy in our trials, but remember that this death only lasts until you get to the other side, for it is then that you discover life.

When God's promise introduces his plan, it stirs up faith's potential.

Day 49

Sanctification

And such were some of you: but ye are washed, but ye are sanctified, but ye are justified in the name of the Lord Jesus, and by the Spirit of our God (1 Corinthians 6:11).

Before God saved us we were among some of the most scandalous people upon the earth serving sin. We were among other things fornicators, lesbians, homosexuals, thieves, liars, cheats, adulterers, covetous, drunkards, party animals and you name it. However, God in his grace saved us and cleaned us up so that we are not the same. It is a settled fact that we have been washed, sanctified, and justified in the name of the Lord Jesus and by the Spirit of our God. However, we still live in the flesh and have not made it to heaven just yet. Although we have been born of an incorruptible seed we still have to wash daily. Neglecting to cleanse yourself daily with the word is like going to the bathroom and forgetting to wipe yourself. Only children neglect to wipe themselves because they are comfortable with the smell. Let us not forget that we are in this world but not of this world. What this means is that we are constantly being inundated and exposed to the god of this world who is also the father of lies. Let us not forget that our spirits are seated with Jesus in heavenly places, far above this world's system of power, might and every name that is named. However, our mind has to constantly be renewed, reminded, and restored to the truth of God's word. It is therefore necessary to fast, come to church, hear the word, and cry unto the Lord our God so that the truth will sink into our spirits while cleansing our minds. We are sanctified and kept by the truth, and his word is truth. In other words we are cleansed by his word. Just as Jesus was sent into the world to save it, we too have been sent for the same reason. This means that although we are like new cars, we will get dirty. It is for this reason that God sanctifies and cleanses us with the washing of the water by the word. The purpose of our cleansing is so that he might present us to himself as a glorious church, not having spot, wrinkle or any such thing. He gives us a spot free wash so that we appear before him holy and without blemish. God wants us to be clean just as He is, for both he that sanctifieth and they who are sanctified are all of one; and it is for this cause he is not ashamed to call us brethren. Under the old covenant the blood of bulls and goats, and the ashes of a heifer would be sprinkled on the unclean. Then sanctified to the purifying of their flesh. So how much more shall the blood of Christ, who through the eternal Spirit offered himself without spot to God. How much more shall he be able to purge your conscience from dead works to serve the living God? What a good question. Think of our sanctification as the process used to make a new car. New steel or sheet metal is forged together to make a car but to insure that it doesn't rust or deteriorate it is sprayed with rustoleum and then painted to protect its look and finish. Our sanctification is like the paint; though the same car gets washed over and over from the dirt it picks up on the road. It is the initial protection that protects the finish. Similarly we were sanctified through the offering of the body of Jesus Christ once for all. For by the one offering he hath perfected for ever them that are sanctified through faith in his blood. When the heart and the mouth connect with the Word it produces righteousness. This has to do with what you think, say, and do for God, through Him. By the word of our mouth we are able to cast down imaginations and bring every thought into the captivity and obedience of Christ. God has called us to salvation through sanctification of the Spirit and belief of the truth. Remember that sanctification makes your salvation work properly. So don't let the same sins plague you.

Whenever the victory of faith is declared, defeat is not an option.

Day 50

The Other Side

And straightway he constrained his disciples to get into the ship, and to go to the other side before unto Bethsaida, while he sent away the people. (Mark 6:45)

Jesus is trying to tell us today to go to the other side of our cross and our trial. We seem to always find ourselves on the wrong side, but Jesus is still encouraging us through his forgiveness. Remember we are only tempted by something that we think will make us wealthy or give us pleasure. Wealth is valuable products, contents, or whatever makes your soul fat and brings satisfaction. This means that wealth is simply a state mind. You might say that wealth is whatever floats your boat. Some people are made wealthy by the prospect of a godly husband or mate. They will be quick to tell you too that if they had a choice between money or a spouse, keep the money, just give me a spouse that is sent from God. Others will say keep the mate, just give me the money. Again you are only tempted by something that you think will make you wealthy. This is the time that a consecrated life comes into play because it enables you to remember the Lord your God. The Holy Spirit will remind you that it is He that gives you the power to get wealth and that wealth is to establish his covenant. Yes, God wants you to remember above all things that He wants to make you wealthy. However, one of the most important things to come to grips with is this, as a man thinks in his heart, so is he. This means that a person is only as wealthy as he thinks that he is. God gives us the power to get wealth, but that power is simply obedience. He gives us the opportunity to be obedient to his word. We must therefore prove ourselves faithful in obedience before God will commit to our trust the true riches. The true riches have to do with the souls of men, which is one of the most valuable resources in heaven or earth. So before God releases them into your hands he is looking to find out what you will do with what we have. What will you do with obedience, for it is the power to get wealth. Now even though Jesus was a son, He had to learn obedience, for he was both God and man. What this means for us is that even though you are a new creature it is important to understand that your mind has to learn or discover what your new creature already knows. For those of you who are struggling to obey God, it is important to know that obedience is learned by the things that you suffer in order to please God. Consequently, without faith in God's discretion, it is impossible to please him. Your mind, which is in the process of being renewed, can never be renewed until you decide to allow the will of your flesh to suffer. So just as Christ suffered for us in the flesh, we must arm ourselves likewise with the same mind. It is when we decide to suffer in the will of our flesh that we cease to sin. We must emphatically declare that we will not live the rest of our time in the lusts of our flesh, but in the will of God. Knowing this, that we can't serve two masters. We will either hate the one and love the other, or we will cling to the one and despise the other.

Now those who belong to God must believe that there is a reward for anything that he asks you to suffer. There is a reward on the other side of your test that is greater and more fulfilling than the pleasure and satisfaction that only lasts for a season. The place where you have continually failed God is only a few steps away from a blessing beyond your imagination. It is only a few steps away from the fullness of joy and complete victory over the will of the flesh. If you are going to realize victory over sin and properly possess your vessel, then you must pass the Garden test. You must learn to recognize the place of your Garden of Gethsemane and spring into action. This starts with praying that you don't enter into temptation, because every person is only tempted when they are drawn away of their own lusts. We can see from the scriptures of Jesus in the Garden of Gethsemane that sometimes our souls are in agony and it becomes necessary to pray more earnestly, or pray again. Yes, before you enter the sin again, wait and pray. When it seems that you are in your greatest trial that God is withdrawn from you, please know that he is only a stone's throw away. One of the things that are commonly overlooked in the hour of temptation is that the Spirit of God is willing and able to keep you when the flesh is weak. His strength actually manifests or comes to its full potential in our weakness. The key is learning how to drink the cup of suffering so that the real you may live. Jesus actually died in the garden before he even made it to the cross. He told the disciples that his soul was dying of sorrow, and so it was the garden death that made dying on the cross possible. This is not a one shot deal, we must continue bearing about the dying of the Lord, so that his life will manifest in us. We have been called to die daily and be crucified realizing that not even the death of Jesus was instant. He died slowly and nothing put him out of his misery. So it is that we must also hang and abide before the Father ever dying or suffering with him. When will we finally understand that he that allows the will of his flesh to suffer will cease from sin? It is when we do decide to suffer that angels will be dispatched to strengthen us. When we suffer with him we are glorified together. We experience what it means to be seated with him in heavenly places far above principalities, powers, dominion, might, and every trial named. The Apostle Paul declared that the sufferings of this present time were not worthy to be compared with the glory which shall be revealed in us. Therefore, if we suffer with him in our trials, God promises that we will reign together.

Faith comes because you recognize that it is God talking.

OTHER BOOKS BY
FRANK THOMPSON

Think Like A Champion – Act Like Goliath

Think Like A Champion is an ancient story with a timeless principle that flips the script on what a real champion looks like, talks like, and how he acts. It shifts the attention from an anointed shepherd boy to the giant that lives inside of us, waiting to overcome the obstacles that he or she may be facing. Opening the contents of this book is sure to inspire and unlock the authority of all believers and launch them into victory so that they "Think Like A Champion".

The Second Half – 21 Days Of Promise
For The Best Days Of Your Life

Are you ready for the second half of your life? Please know that God does not want you agonizing over the past, or concentrating on the things of old. He is about to do a new thing in your life as you realize that halftime is over, and that it is time for the second half. It's time to get ready for a new beginning. A new beginning is the start of something fresh, exciting, and great from God. Whenever God gets ready to give you a new beginning, he will always give you a promise. A promise is simply an announcement of blessing and provision with a pledge from Him to carry it out. The announcement will always have instructions for manifestation. This book of 21 promises sets in motion a word from God, and confessions to live by as you prepare for the best days of your life.

Prayer On The Go For Men

Statistics tell us that most men have not depended on prayer as their main resource for answers in the past, and the present doesn't look much better. However, all of heaven and hell have targeted their thought life and its mode of operation. Yes, your thought life is the key to your healing, success, and financial deliverance. Therefore God wants to change the way that you think about prayer, and give you a future that is shaped and molded by the confidence that is in its reward.

For a list of materials from Frank Thompson Ministries, please contact the ministry at the following address:

Frank Thompson Ministries
6301 Garfield
Berkeley, MO 63134
314-486-9911

Made in the USA
Las Vegas, NV
26 August 2022

54035390R00083